A LIFEGUIDE BIBLE STUDY

ROMANS
Becoming New in Christ
21 Studies in 2 Parts
for individuals or groups
Jack Kuhatschek

With Notes for Leaders

INTERVARSITY PRESS
DOWNERS GROVE, ILLINOIS 60515

InterVarsity Press® is the book-publishing division of InterVarsity Christian Fellowship®, a student movement active on campus at hundreds of universities, colleges and schools of nursing in the United States of America, and a member movement of the International Fellowship of Evangelical Students. For information about local and regional activities, write Public Relations Dept., InterVarsity Christian Fellowship, 6400 Schroeder Rd., P.O. Box 7895, Madison, WI 53707-7895.

LifeGuide® is a registered trademark of InterVarsity Christian Fellowship.

Cover photograph: Robert McKendrick

ISBN 0-8308-1008-0

Printed in the United States of America ♾

32	31	30	29	28	27	26	25	24	23	22	21	20	19	18	17
10	09	08	07	06	05	04	03	02	01	00	99	98	97	96	95

Contents

Getting the Most
from LifeGuide Bible Studies

Many of us long to fill our minds and our lives with Scripture. We desire to be transformed by its message. LifeGuide Bible Studies are designed to be an exciting and challenging way to do just that. They help us to be guided by God's Word in every area of life.

How They Work

LifeGuides have a number of distinctive features. Perhaps the most important is that they are *inductive* rather than *deductive*. In other words, they lead us to *discover* what the Bible says rather than simply *telling* us what it says.

They are also thought provoking. They help us to think about the meaning of the passage so that we can truly understand what the author is saying. The questions require more than one-word answers.

The studies are personal. Questions expose us to the promises, assurances, exhortations and challenges of God's Word. They are designed to allow the Scriptures to renew our minds so that we can be transformed by the Spirit of God. This is the ultimate goal of all Bible study.

The studies are versatile. They are designed for student, neighborhood and church groups. They are also effective for individual study.

How They're Put Together

LifeGuides also have a distinctive format. Each study need take no more than forty-five minutes in a group setting or thirty minutes in personal study—unless you choose to take more time.

The studies can be used within a quarter system in a church and fit well in a semester or trimester system on a college campus. If a guide has more than thirteen studies, it is divided into two or occasionally three parts of approximately twelve studies each.

LifeGuides use a workbook format. Space is provided for writing answers to each question. This is ideal for personal study and allows group members to prepare in advance for the discussion.

The studies also contain leader's notes. They show how to lead a group discussion, provide additional background information on certain questions, give helpful tips on group dynamics and suggest ways to deal with problems which may arise during the discussion. With such helps, someone with little or no experience can lead an effective study.

Suggestions for Individual Study

1. As you begin each study, pray that God will help you to understand and apply the passage to your life.

2. Read and reread the assigned Bible passage to familiarize yourself with what the author is saying. In the case of book studies, you may want to read through the entire book prior to the first study. This will give you a helpful overview of its contents.

3. A good modern translation of the Bible, rather than the King James Version or a paraphrase, will give you the most help. The New International Version, the New American Standard Bible and the Revised Standard Version are all recommended. However, the questions in this guide are based on the New International Version.

4. Write your answers in the space provided in the study guide. This will help you to express your understanding of the passage clearly.

5. It might be good to have a Bible dictionary handy. Use it to look up any unfamiliar words, names or places.

Suggestions for Group Study

1. Come to the study prepared. Follow the suggestions for individual study mentioned above. You will find that careful preparation will greatly enrich your time spent in group discussion.

2. Be willing to participate in the discussion. The leader of your group will not be lecturing. Instead, he or she will be encouraging the members of the group to discuss what they have learned from the passage. The leader will be asking the questions that are found in this guide. Plan to share what God has taught you in your individual study.

3. Stick to the passage being studied. Your answers should be based on the verses which are the focus of the discussion and not on outside authorities such as commentaries or speakers. This guide deliberately avoids jumping

from book to book or passage to passage. Each study focuses on only one passage. Book studies are generally designed to lead you through the book in the order in which it was written. This will help you follow the author's argument.

4. Be sensitive to the other members of the group. Listen attentively when they share what they have learned. You may be surprised by their insights! Link what you say to the comments of others so the group stays on the topic. Also, be affirming whenever you can. This will encourage some of the more hesitant members of the group to participate.

5. Be careful not to dominate the discussion. We are sometimes so eager to share what we have learned that we leave too little opportunity for others to respond. By all means participate! But allow others to also.

6. Expect God to teach you through the passage being discussed and through the other members of the group. Pray that you will have an enjoyable and profitable time together.

7. If you are the discussion leader, you will find additional suggestions and helpful ideas for each study in the leader's notes. These are found at the back of the guide.

Introducing Romans

Romans may be the most important letter you will ever read. It is Paul's masterpiece, the clearest and fullest explanation of the gospel in the Bible. John Calvin said that "if a man understands it, he has a sure road opened for him to the understanding of the whole Scripture." William Tyndale, the father of English Bible translators, believed that every Christian should learn it by heart. "The more it is studied," he wrote, "the easier it is; the more it is chewed, the pleasanter it is" (Prologue to Romans in his 1534 English New Testament).

But watch out! Those who study Romans are rarely the same afterward. For example, in the summer of A.D. 386 Augustine sat weeping in the garden of his friend Alypius. He wanted to begin a new life but lacked the strength to break with the old. Taking up a scroll of Romans, he read the words, "Put on the Lord Jesus Christ and make no provision for the flesh in regard to its lusts." "No further would I read," he tells us, "nor had I any need; instantly at the end of this sentence, a clear light flooded my heart and all the darkness of doubt vanished away."

In 1515 Martin Luther began to teach the book of Romans to his students. He wrote, "Night and day I pondered until . . . I grasped the truth that the righteousness of God is that righteousness whereby, through grace and sheer mercy, he justifies us by faith. Thereupon I felt myself to be reborn and to have gone through open doors into paradise. The whole scripture took on new meaning, and whereas before the 'righteousness of God' had filled me with hate, now it became to me inexpressibly sweet in greater love. This passage in Paul became to me a gateway to heaven." Two years later he nailed his ninety-five theses on the door of the Castle church in Wittenberg, and the Protestant Reformation began!

The evening of May 24, 1738, John Wesley "went very unwillingly to a society in Aldersgate Street, where one was reading Luther's preface to the Epistle to the Romans. About a quarter before nine," he wrote in his journal, "while he was describing the change which God works in the heart through faith in Christ, I felt my heart strangely warmed. I felt I did trust in Christ, Christ alone, for my salvation; and an assurance was given me that he had taken *my* sins away, even *mine;* and saved me from the law of sin and death." This event in Wesley's life helped to launch the great Evangelical Revival of the eighteenth century.

We need to grasp the message of Romans in our day as well. Many are preaching a gospel which lacks clarity and substance. People are told to "invite Jesus into their heart" or simply to "follow Christ" without understanding the meaning of his death and resurrection.

We cannot correct this problem merely by memorizing gospel outlines or canned presentations. We need to immerse ourselves in Scripture through diligent study and thoughtful reflection. Only when the gospel grips us as it did Augustine, Luther and Wesley will we realize why "it is the power of God for the salvation of everyone who believes" (Rom 1:16).

Romans is different from most of Paul's other letters. He did not found the church in Rome; in fact, he had never even been there. It has been suggested that the church in Rome was founded by some of those who were present on the day of Pentecost (Acts 2:10). However, Paul had met some of the Christians in Rome, such as Priscilla and Aquila (Rom 16), during his missionary journeys to other cities.

Other letters were written to address specific problems within the churches. Romans seems relatively free of problems. Their only major "problem" was that they had never met the apostle. Therefore, he felt a need to fully explain to them in a letter what he normally would have said in person.

Paul probably wrote Romans between A.D. 57-58 while he was at Corinth in the home of his friend and convert Gaius. He planned to go first to Jerusalem to deliver a gift of money from the gentile churches to the poor in Jerusalem. Then he hoped to visit Rome on his way to Spain. His hopes were later realized, but not as he had expected. When he finally arrived in Rome in early A.D. 60, he was a prisoner under house arrest (Acts 28:11-31).

This study guide is written in two parts. Part 1 contains twelve studies which look at Romans 1—8. Study 12 reviews these chapters. Part 2 contains nine studies which cover Romans 9—16. Study 9 is also a review.

May you be encouraged and challenged by the new life and the new lifestyle we have in Christ!

Part 1
A New Life

Romans 1—8

1
Good News from God

Romans 1:1-17

I'm engaged!"
"I got a raise!"
"My wife's having a baby!"

What is our immediate response to good news? We tell others! We feel we will burst unless we share our joy with those around us.

Paul felt that way about the gospel, the good news about Jesus Christ. As we read these opening verses in his letter to the Romans, we find his excitement is contagious.

---

1. Why is it so difficult to keep good news to ourselves?

It is uplifting to hear good news and people like to spread good cheer by telling good news to EVERYONE.

---

2. Read Romans 1:1-17. Imagine that verses 1 and 5 are the only information you possess about Paul. Describe everything you would know about him.

Paul is a ALL Rightous dude, Devoted Servant of Jesus Christ.

---

3. In verses 1-5 Paul gives a summary of the gospel for which he had been set apart. What do we learn about the gospel from these verses?

4. What do verses 8-13 reveal about Paul's attitude toward the Romans?

Paul loved the Romanse, he wanted to come and see them, to save them and to add more faith to their hearts enabling to be obedient servants, but God didn't open the door until Paul knew that there will be a good harvest

Why do you think he was so encouraged and motivated?

Paul had a great desire to share with the Romanse about the good news, and to build a strong faith in their hearts towards God.

---

5. Because he was an apostle ("one who is sent"), Paul felt obligated to preach the gospel to everyone (v. 14). Whom do you have the greatest opportunity of reaching with the gospel?

To To Evrey body

---

6. What steps can you take to reach them?

By Love and by Living

---

7. Paul says we can be eager to preach the gospel or be ashamed of it (vv. 15-16). What might lead us to adopt one attitude or the other?

① Because he was obligated towards obidient to God's will
② Ashamed shows disobedient.

---

8. In verse 16 Paul describes the gospel as "the power of God" for salvation. How have you seen this power demonstrated in your life or the lives of others?

by Seeing unrighteousenss because righteousenss

9. Martin Luther wrote that verse 17 became to him "a gateway to heaven."
What's so significant about the ideas in this verse?

That Righteouseness and faith are the significant
reaquirment for God's will.

---

10. Pray that God will use Romans to give you Paul's attitude toward the
gospel and toward those who need its message.

2
The Wrath of God
Romans 1:18-32

Now are you?" someone asks. "I'm fine," we reply. But are we really, or do our words mask our true condition? In this passage Paul tells us that we are not fine—neither we nor our friends nor society. Something is dreadfully wrong.

1. Usually we have to admit we need help before we can be helped. Why do we often find it so difficult to admit a need?

Admites of weakness, and old nature took place.

2. Read Romans 1:18-32. John Stott defines God's wrath (v. 18) as "his righteous reaction to evil, his implacable hostility to it, his refusal to condone it, and his judgment upon it."[1] According to this definition, how would God's wrath differ from the sinful anger or violent temper condemned by Scripture?

is love for evil people he let them make their own disesion, God reveal himself pretty well to the people, enabling to understand the diffirence between Good and evil.

3. What does everyone know about God, according to verses 19-20?

We Know that God is existing, through Meracles that's why no excuse for those who deny God's existence.

How do they know these things?

Every day's life Meracles observing, watching God at work and try to Joine him.

4. How do people respond to the knowledge they possess about God (vv. 18, 21)? *By knowing that he is existing but denying and ignoring him and not thanking him or worshiping hi*

5. Verses 21-32 describe the downward spiral of sin experienced by people who rebel against God. How would you summarize each level of their descent? *When the man loses God he loses everything and he stumble and fall, then getting worse Accordingly*

How might each level lead to the next? *When they stumble, they lose God, then themselves, family, became God's haiters eregant, doing evil thing and although they know th it's against God's will, but they enjoy doing it.*

6. What evidence do you see of this moral and spiritual degeneration today? *No formal religion at all now in life, they sent bik away from schools,*

7. It is common to think of God's wrath primarily in terms of future judgment. Yet verse 18 states that God's wrath is now being revealed. How is this evident from verses 24-32? *He gave them over to the discive of their hearts, but they trated the truth of God to lies*

8. Do you think verses 18-32 refute the notion that people are basically good? Explain. Because General Consept man is not good for not accepting God's will, So God turned his face away, and saten will Control men and will fill all gabs.

9. People often raise the question of how God could condemn those who have never heard of him. How does this passage address this question?

No exceouse for not Knowing God, because he revealed himself in So many ways-

10. How might this passage make you less ashamed of the gospel and more eager to preach it? Negatiue, we are not ashoune because people were foolish, and positive part you have Compasion to the people that's Why you will hawe more eager to preach it.

¹John R. W. Stott, "God's Judgment" in *Believing and Obeying Jesus Christ* (Downers Grove, Ill.: InterVarsity Press, 1980), p. 48.

3
The Judgment of God

Romans 2:1-29

Prostitutes, drug addicts, thieves—it's easy to see why these people need the gospel. But what about "respectable" people: doctors, business executives, the family next door? They seem so contented, so fulfilled, so . . . *nice!*

In Romans 1:18-32 Paul described the depravity of those who reject God. Now he imagines someone saying, "You're absolutely right, Paul. Such people are wicked and deserve everything that's coming to them! But of course *we* would never do such things and would be very critical of anyone who did." In this passage Paul shows why even "nice" people need the gospel.

1. Have you ever wondered whether some non-Christians really need the gospel? Explain.

2. Read Romans 2:1-29. When people are judgmental of others, how do they reveal both an understanding and a misunderstanding of God's judgment (vv. 1-4)?

3. Explain why God's kindness might lead them to be either repentant or presumptuous (v. 4).

4. Verses 5-16 describe a future day of judgment known as "the day of God's wrath" (v. 5). What will God consider important and unimportant on that day?

5. How are God's standards of judgment both similar and different for the two groups described in verses 12-16?

6. Many non-Christians have high moral standards. How can we use their own standards to help them see their need of Christ?

7. In verses 17-29 Paul focuses his attention on a hypocritical Jew. How does such a person view himself and others (vv. 17-20)?

8. Why would non-Jews blaspheme God's name because of such people (vv. 21-24)?

9. How has religious hypocrisy hurt the cause of Christ in our day?

10. Jews placed great value on circumcision because it was the visible sign that they were God's people. How had some of them confused the sign with what it signified (vv. 25-29)?

11. How might religious people today have a similar misunderstanding about baptism or some other ritual or practice?

12. How can this chapter help us to more effectively share the gospel with respectable, religious or moral non-Christians?

4
The
Verdict

Romans 3:1-20

If your eternal destiny were decided by the quality of your life and the level of your obedience to God, how would you fare? There is one sure way to find out. Take your case to the divine court. The Bible assures us that we will all have our day in court (Rom 2:5-6; 14:10-12). But we need not wait until then to find out the verdict. Paul tells us in advance in this passage.

1. Describe some of the thoughts and feelings you might have if you were on trial for committing a serious crime—and you knew you were guilty.

2. Read Romans 3:1-20. What were some of the spiritual advantages in being a Jew?

3. Why might some Jews have accused God of unfaithfulness and injustice (vv. 3-8)?

How does Paul respond to these accusations?

4. What are some of the religious advantages God has granted to you?

How have they helped you?

5. In the role of prosecutor, Paul has charged that Jews and Gentiles alike are under sin (v. 9). How does Scripture support his charge (vv. 10-18)?

6. In verses 13-18 Paul describes how the various parts of our bodies are involved in sin. How does this figurative language graphically illustrate our condition as fallen people?

7. How would you reconcile the statements in verses 10-18 with the fact that some non-Christians *do* seem to seek after God and lead exemplary lives?

8. Imagine a courtroom scene with God as the judge and the world on trial. From what you have learned in Romans 1:18—3:20, summarize the charges against us, the supporting evidence and the verdict.

9. Paul does not discuss the grace of God (3:21—5:21) until he has discussed the judgment of God (1:18—3:20). He does not proclaim the good news until we have understood the bad news. Why does he follow this order?

How should Paul's example affect our evangelism? (Be as specific as possible.)

10. The letter to the Romans could have ended with 3:20. God would be perfectly just to condemn us all and to leave us fearfully awaiting his wrath. Let this fact sink in for a moment, then take time to thank God for not only being just, but also merciful and gracious.

5
The Righteousness from God

Romans 3:21-31

Like prisoners on death row, people are guilty, condemned and awaiting the execution of God's wrath. They sit silently in the miserable darkness of their cell, all hope extinguished.

Then abruptly, the door swings open and darkness becomes light, death becomes life, and bondage becomes freedom. "You are *pardoned*," a voice tells them. But how? Why? This passage answers these questions.

1. Imagine that you are a judge and someone you love is on trial. Would you be more tempted to compromise your justice or your love? Explain.

2. How is the righteousness from God (3:22-24) different from righteousness by law (2:5-13)?

3. What does it mean to have faith in Jesus Christ (v. 22)?

4. In verses 24-25 Paul uses three important words to describe what Christ has done for us. The word *justified* (v. 24) is borrowed from the law court. The judge declares that the person on trial has no legal charges against him. Why is our justification remarkable, given the background of Romans 1:18—3:20?

5. How should our complete acceptance by God affect the way we view ourselves?

6. The word *redemption* (v. 24) is borrowed from the slave market. It means to buy someone out of slavery. From what types of slavery has Christ delivered us?

7. The phrase *sacrifice of atonement* (v. 25) is borrowed from the Old Testament. Animal sacrifices turned away God's wrath from the sinner. Why does Christ's death turn away God's wrath from us?

How should we respond, emotionally and spiritually, to the fact that Jesus experienced God's wrath for us?

8. Some people find it difficult to understand how God can be perfectly just and gracious at the same time. How do the justice and grace of God meet at the cross (vv. 25-26)?

9. How does boasting about ourselves betray a fundamental misunderstanding of the gospel (vv. 27-31)?

10. At times do you still feel unacceptable to God? Explain.

11. In what ways might you feel or act differently if you more fully grasped what Jesus has done for you?

12. Take time to praise and thank God for Jesus Christ.

6
The Example of Abraham

Romans 4:1-25

Lt's hopeless." No words are more discouraging than these. Yet sometimes situations appear beyond hope, beyond help. Our natural response during such times is despair and depression.

Abraham knew what it meant to face insurmountable obstacles. He too was hopeless, yet somehow found renewed reason to hope. For this reason he has become a timeless example and encouragement for us.

1. Briefly describe a situation in which you felt hopeless.

2. Read Romans 4. According to Paul, how were Old Testament saints, such as Abraham and David, justified (vv. 1-8)?

How do we know this?

3. What are some of the differences between justification by faith and by works (vv. 4-8)?

4. It's easy to feel that God accepts us only when we are good. When we feel this way, how can the examples of Abraham and David give us hope?

5. Some people in Paul's day taught that unless a person was circumcised he had no hope of being saved (see Acts 15:1). How does Abraham's experience refute this idea (vv. 9-12)?

6. Some people today claim that unless we are baptized we have no hope of being saved. How might Abraham's experience refute this claim?

7. God promised that Abraham and his offspring would inherit the world (v. 13). Who are Abraham's offspring (vv. 13-17)?

What difference does it make whether the promise to Abraham and his offspring is fulfilled by law or grace?

8. Paul states that the God in whom Abraham believed "gives life to the dead and calls things that are not as though they were" (v. 17). How does this statement relate to Abraham's predicament described in verses 18-22?

9. How does Abraham illustrate our own hopeless predicament as non-Christians and the solution provided in Jesus Christ (vv. 18-25)?

10. What situation are you currently facing which requires faith in the God of resurrection and creation?

11. How can you demonstrate faith and hope in that situation?

7
Reasons to Rejoice
Romans 5:1-21

We all long to be joyful, to experience the pure delight that life sometimes offers. But life's joys are elusive, momentary, gone as quickly as they come. How can we have an abiding, enduring joy—especially when suffering intrudes into our lives? In Romans 5 Paul gives us several firm and lasting reasons to rejoice.

1. What kinds of things make you joyful?

2. Read Romans 5:1-11. How has faith in Jesus Christ changed our relationship with God (vv. 1-2)?

3. In verses 2-11 what reasons does Paul give for rejoicing?

4. What does it mean to "rejoice in the hope of the glory of God" (v. 2)?

How has this been a source of joy to you?

5. How does suffering for Christ's sake produce the character changes mentioned in verses 3-4?

6. How can a knowledge of this process help us to rejoice in our sufferings?

7. How do verses 5-8 emphasize the love God has for us?

8. How do verses 9-10 assure us that God accepts us completely in Christ?

9. Why should God's outpouring of love and his complete acceptance make us rejoice (v. 11)?

10. Read verses 12-21. How are Adam and Christ similar (vv. 12, 18-19)?

11. How is Christ's gift different from Adam's trespass (vv. 15-21)?

12. This passage gives us many reasons for rejoicing. Spend time thanking and praising God for all we have in Jesus Christ.

8
New Life, New Lifestyle

Romans 6:1—7:6

Subtle allure, persistent urges, passionate desires. Sin entices us in many ways. A thought enters our mind which we dare not acknowledge: "If I give in, I can always be forgiven." Sound familiar? Such thinking can become an excuse for immoral practices. But it betrays a fundamental misunderstanding of God's grace in our lives. In Romans 6:1—7:6 Paul explains why the idea of "sinning so that grace may increase" is unthinkable for Christians.

1. When you became a Christian, was the change in your life dramatic, gradual or imperceptible? Explain.

2. Read Romans 6:1-14. In what sense was our baptism both a funeral and a resurrection (vv. 1-4)?

3. Our "old self" (v. 6) refers to everything we were as non-Christians. When our old self was crucified with Christ, in what sense was sin rendered powerless (vv. 5-7)?

4. If sin has been rendered powerless and we have been freed from sin, then why do we still sin?

5. Sin reigns over a person until death. How has Christ freed us from this tyranny (vv. 8-11)?

6. What does it mean to "count yourselves dead to sin but alive to God" (v. 11)?

7. If we realize sin is no longer our master, how should our lives be different (vv. 12-14)?

8. Read Romans 6:15-23. Paul compares both our old life and our new to slavery. Why is this analogy appropriate in each case (vv. 15-18)?

9. How does our slavery to God differ from our slavery to sin (vv. 19-23)?

10. Read Romans 7:1-6. How is the principle "that the law has authority over a man only as long as he lives" illustrated by marriage (vv. 1-3)?

How does this apply to our relationship with the law and with Christ (vv. 4-6)?

11. In 6:1—7:6 Paul uses baptism, slavery and marriage to illustrate the differences between our old life and our new life. What common themes are emphasized in these illustrations?

12. What assurance and encouragement is Paul giving us in our struggle against sin?

9
Our Struggle with Sin

Romans 7:7-25

Are you ever baffled by your behavior? You know the right thing to do, but you fail to do it. You resolve to avoid certain things, and they become even more attractive and enticing. Why? What keeps us from translating our desires into actions?

In Romans 7 Paul explores his own inner struggles to do good and avoid evil. As we look into his mind and heart, we see a reflection of ourselves and the power that opposes us.

1. Saying no to a piece of pie we don't need *seems* so simple but is easier said than done. Why is it often such a struggle to do what we know we should do?

2. Read Romans 7:7-12. Paul opens this section by asking if the law is sin (v. 7). What has he said previously which might lead to that conclusion?

3. How did the law create in Paul a vivid awareness of sin?

4. Why then is it wrong to blame the law for our sinful behavior?

5. Read verses 13-25. Why would it also be wrong to blame the law for Paul's spiritual death (vv. 13-14)?

6. According to verses 14-20, why does Paul feel so wretched?

7. In chapter 6 Paul stated that Christians are no longer slaves to sin. Yet here he claims he is a slave to sin (v. 14). How would you explain this difference?

8. To what extent can you identify with Paul's struggles in these verses? Explain.

9. Paul compares his struggle with sin to a war, with sin as the aggressor (v. 23). Describe the nature and outcome of this war (vv. 21-23).

10. How can a person's anguish and frustration with sin be beneficial (vv. 24-25)?

11. Why is it important to realize that only Christ can rescue us from the power of sin?

12. When Paul realized that Jesus could rescue him from his wretched condition, he cried out, "Thanks be to God!" If this is your response too, spend time thanking him.

10
The Spirit Brings Life

Romans 8:1-17

If we were unable to obey God as non-Christians, then how can we as Christians? What has happened to turn our slavery into freedom, our sin into righteousness and our spiritual death into life?

The struggle described in Romans 7 does not end when we become Christians. But there is a new dimension to that struggle which totally changes its outcome. In chapter 8 Paul describes the life-giving effects of the Spirit.

1. The Holy Spirit brings life to every Christian at the moment of conversion. What were some early signs of life when you became a Christian?

2. Read Romans 8:1-17. Romans 7 described how the law of sin brought about our spiritual death. What has God done to free us from the law of sin and death (vv. 1-4)?

3. How does this affect the outcome of our struggle with sin described in 7:13-25?

4. In verses 5-8 Paul divides all of humanity into two categories: those who live according to the sinful nature and those who live according to the Spirit. In your own words, what are some characteristics of each group?

According to verse 9, how do we know which category we are in?

5. There are many professing Christians whose lives seem very different from Paul's description of life in the Spirit. How do you think Paul would account for this fact?

6. What evidence do you see of your life being controlled by the Spirit?

7. What are the results of having the Spirit live in us (vv. 10-11)?

8. In verse 12 Paul concludes that we have an obligation. Describe in your own words the negative and positive aspects of that obligation (vv. 12-14).

9. Paul states that "if you live according to the sinful nature, you will die" (v. 13). How can this be reconciled with his teaching on justification by faith?

10. Practically speaking, what does it mean to put to death the misdeeds of the body by the Spirit (vv. 13-14)?

11. How do we experience the reality and privileges of being God's children (vv. 15-17)?

12. Spend time thanking God for the gift of the Spirit and the difference he makes in our lives.

11
Glorious Conquerors
Romans 8:18-39

R oman conquerors returning from the wars enjoyed the honor of a triumph, a tumultuous parade. In the procession came trumpeters, musicians and strange animals from the conquered territories, together with carts laden with treasure and captured armaments. The conqueror rode in a triumphal chariot, the dazed prisoners walking in chains before him. Sometimes his children, robed in white, stood with him in the chariot or rode the trace horses. A slave stood behind the conqueror, holding a golden crown and whispering in his ear a warning: that all glory is fleeting."*

In Romans 8 Paul describes Christians as glorious conquerors, who by God's grace overcome all forces arrayed against us. But the glory we receive is eternal.

1. Why is it often difficult to feel like a glorious conqueror?

2. Read Romans 8:18-27. What words and vivid images in these verses underscore the difficulties of the present time?

3. Explain why these difficulties don't compare with the glory that will be revealed in us.

4. How can this eager expectation help us cope with our present problems and sufferings?

5. How can the Spirit's help also encourage us (vv. 26-27)?

6. Read verses 28-39. How would you describe the mood of these verses?

7. In verse 28 Paul speaks of "the good" and "his purpose." What is God's good purpose for us (v. 29)?

8. How do the words *foreknew, predestined, called, justified* and *glorified* help us understand how God accomplishes his purpose for us?

9. Paul asks: "What, then, shall we say in response to this?" (v. 31). How are you encouraged by Paul's answer (vv. 31-32)?

10. In verses 33-34 Paul imagines a courtroom in which God is the judge and Jesus is our defense attorney. How and why would they reply to any charges brought against us?

11. How might trouble, hardship, persecution, famine, nakedness, danger or the threat of death cause us to question God's love for us (vv. 35-36)?

12. In spite of these things, why does Paul proclaim that we are "more than conquerors" (vv. 37-39)?

13. In verse 17 Paul stated that we must share in Christ's sufferings in order to share in his glory. How does this passage clarify and confirm this fact?

*At the end of the movie *Patton,* these words went through the mind of that famous general.

12
Review

Romans 1—8

Facts are funny things—so difficult to learn, so easily forgotten. We quickly forget far more than we remember. But a review can help. It puts things back into the "active file" of our brains. It enables us to sort out and organize new information, making it more accessible and usable. A good review reinforces learning. This study helps you review the first eight chapters of Romans.

1. What are some reasons why people today are ashamed to preach the gospel?

2. Which of these reasons do you struggle with the most?

3. How can Paul's discussion in Romans 1—8 help you to feel unashamed in this area, even *eager* to preach the gospel?

4. If you were to present the gospel to someone, using chapters 1—5 as the basis of your presentation, what would be the most important items for you to discuss?

5. Imagine that you are counseling a Christian who feels enslaved to a sinful habit. What might you say to him or her from Romans 6—8?

6. According to Paul, what are some reasons why we can expect suffering to be a normal part of our Christian experience?

7. What present and future reasons do we have for rejoicing?

8. In 1:16 Paul described the gospel as "the power of God." Having studied Romans 1—8, how is that power more evident to you now?

9. Up to this point, what have you enjoyed most about studying Romans?

Part 2
A New Lifestyle
Romans 9—16

1
The Potter and His Clay

Romans 9:1-29

I don't believe in Christ." It grieves us to hear these words. But when they come from close friends or family members, the pain can be unbearable. Why doesn't God open their hearts to the gospel? Why did he save us and not them?

Paul felt great pain and perplexity over Israel's unbelief. Their Messiah had come and they had rejected him. Why had God allowed this to happen? Had he rejected his people? In chapters 9—11 Paul wrestles with these questions. In this chapter his answer focuses on the difficult subject of God's sovereignty.

1. Ten people are guilty of exactly the same crime. The judge decides to pardon all but one, who serves the full sentence. How would you evaluate the judge's decision?

2. Read Romans 9:1-29. Why does Paul have great sorrow for the people of Israel (vv. 1-5)?

3. How do verses 6-13 demonstrate that God has not failed in his promises and purposes for Israel?

4. How do you respond to the idea of election (v. 11), God choosing certain people to be the objects of his mercy?

5. Many people feel it is unjust for God to choose some and not others (v. 14). In reply why does Paul speak of God's mercy rather than his justice or injustice (vv. 15-18)?

6. To what extent can you identify with the objection raised in verse 19?

7. How does the illustration of the potter and his clay help us gain a proper perspective (vv. 20-23)?

8. How is God's mercy and justice revealed in his treatment of the Gentiles and Jews (vv. 24-29)?

9. A story has been told that when we approach the gates of heaven we will read, "Whoever wishes may enter." Yet as we pass through the gates and look back, we will read, "Chosen before the foundation of the world." Do you find this story helpful or not? Explain.

10. Thank God for the fact that although he would have been perfectly just to condemn us all, he mercifully chose to save some.

2
Misguided Zeal

Romans 9:30—10:21

The world is full of religious people: Jews, Christians, Muslims, Hindus, Buddhists and many others. Islam alone has over 800 million adherents. Many of these people are zealous, dedicated and sincere. But are zeal and sincerity enough? Are there many paths to God or just one?

In this passage Paul continues to wrestle with the problem of Israel's unbelief. Having considered the problem from the standpoint of divine election, he now focuses on Israel's and on our own responsibility to believe the gospel.

1. Have you ever known a sincere and devout non-Christian? How did you respond to his or her zeal?

2. Read Romans 9:30—10:21. Why was Jesus Christ more of a stumbling stone to the Jews than to the Gentiles (9:30-33)?

3. In 10:2 Paul states that the Israelites are "zealous for God." Why doesn't this conflict with what he said about human depravity in 3:10-18?

4. Many people believe religious zeal and sincerity are all a person needs to be saved. How would Paul respond to this belief (10:1-4)?

5. In verses 6-8 Paul rewords Deuteronomy 30:11-14 in order to describe righteousness by faith. How do verses 6-8 stress the simplicity of this righteousness?

How does it differ from righteousness by law (v. 5)?

6. First-century Christians publicly confessed that "Jesus is Lord" at their baptism. Why do you think public confession (vv. 9-13) is important to the belief in one's heart?

7. In what ways have you publicly expressed your belief in Christ?

8. F. F. Bruce writes: "At an earlier stage in Paul's argument [Rom 3:22] the words 'there is no difference' had a grim sound, because they convicted Jew and Gentile together of sin against God."[1] How do these same words now have a joyful sound (vv. 11-13)?

9. William Carey, the father of modern missions, once proposed to a group of ministers that they discuss the implications of the Great Commission. Dr. John C. Ryland retorted: "Young man, sit down. When God pleases to convert the heathen, he will do it without your aid or mine!" How does Dr. Ryland's understanding of God's sovereignty mesh with verses 14-15?

10. Realizing the implications of verses such as Romans 10:14-15, William Carey responded to God's call and went to India. To where do you feel called to go with the gospel?

What steps can you take (or have you taken) to be obedient to that call?

11. What do verses 16-21 reveal about the reasons for Israel's unbelief?

12. Israel's unbelief did not stop Paul from praying for them (10:1). Spend time praying for those with whom you have the opportunity of sharing the gospel.

---

[1]F. F. Bruce, *The Epistle of Paul to the Romans* (Grand Rapids, Mich.: Eerdmans, 1963), p. 202.

3
The Future of Israel

Romans 11:1-36

For centuries the people of Israel awaited their Messiah. But when he came, very few believed in him. This situation has persisted to the point where Christianity is now considered a gentile religion. What happened to God's promises and plans for Israel? Has God rejected his people? In this chapter Paul answers these questions.

1. What difference does it make whether God has rejected Israel?

2. Read Romans 11. How does Paul know that God has not rejected his people (vv. 1-6)?

3. What were the spiritual consequences for those Israelites who rejected Jesus Christ (vv. 7-10)?

Why are these consequences inevitable for anyone who persistently rejects the gospel?

---

4. How did Israel's rejection of Christ result in riches for others (vv. 11-16)?

---

5. Why is Paul convinced that even greater blessings will come from their acceptance of Christ (vv. 11-16)?

---

6. Why should Paul's illustration of the olive tree prevent Gentiles from feeling superior to unbelieving Israelites (vv. 17-24)?

Why is it just as foolish for Christians today to feel superior to non-Christians?

---

7. What does the illustration of the olive tree teach about the relationship between Israel and the church?

8. It is sometimes claimed that God no longer has a special relationship with ethnic Israel. How would you respond to this claim in light of verses 25-32?

9. In this chapter Paul has argued that Israel's unbelief is partial (vv. 1-10), purposeful (vv. 11-16) and temporary (vv. 25-32). How does this make him feel about God (vv. 33-36)?

10. How can Paul's description of God in verses 33-36 also encourage us to trust and praise him?

4
Living
Sacrifices

Romans 12:1-21

In the first eleven chapters Paul has described God's gift of righteousness. In Christ we who were condemned are justified. We who were sinners are sanctified. And we who had no hope will be glorified. But what is our proper response to God's mercy, love and grace? Paul tells us in this and the following chapters.

1. Jesus once told a Pharisee that a person who is forgiven little loves little. But a person who is forgiven much loves much (Lk 7:47). Why do you think this is so?

2. Read Romans 12. What are some ways God's mercy (v. 1) has been demonstrated in Romans 1—11?

3. Why do you think Paul uses the imagery of *living sacrifices* to describe our proper response to God's mercy?

Why do you think this kind of worship is pleasing to God?

---

4. J. B. Phillips paraphrases verse 2 as, "Don't let the world around you squeeze you into its own mold." In what ways are we influenced and pressured to conform to the world?

---

5. What are some ways we can renew our minds (v. 2) and so be transformed?

---

6. Sometimes we view God's will as something to be avoided rather than desired. How can the last part of verse 2 correct this distortion?

---

7. How can the realization that we are members of a body (vv. 3-8) prevent us from thinking too highly of ourselves (v. 3)?

---

8. As you think "with sober judgment" about yourself, what gift (or gifts) do you think God has given you (vv. 3-8)?

How can you use it [them] to benefit the body of Christ?

9. How would the kind of love Paul describes in verses 9-16 transform our relationships with other Christians?

10. How would Paul's advice in verses 17-21 help us to overcome our enemies?

11. In what ways do you need to begin living more sacrificially before God, other Christians or the world?

5
Submitting to Authorities
Romans 13:1-14

The sergeant glares at a delinquent recruit whose face is now only inches away.

"That's an order!" he barks. "Do you understand?"

"Yes, sir," replies the recruit.

"I can't *hear* you!" shouts the sergeant.

"YES, SIR," screams the recruit, who has just had his first lesson in military authority.

For many people the word *authority* conjures up images like the one just described. Those in authority are viewed as oppressors, and too often the impression is correct. Paul was no stranger to the abuses of authority. He had experienced much persecution at the hands of civil and religious authorities all around the Mediterranean. In light of this, Paul's view of authority may be surprising.

---

1. What comes into your mind when you hear the word *authority?*

---

2. Read Romans 3:21-31. How is the righteousness from God (3:22-24) different from righteousness by law (2:5-13)?

3. What is Paul's view of authority and those who exercise it (vv. 1-5)?

4. How would Paul's view of governing authorities apply to wicked and perverse rulers such as Nero or Hitler?

5. What are some reasons Paul gives for submitting to those in authority (vv. 1-5)?

6. Do you think it is ever appropriate to resist rather than to submit to the authorities? Explain.

7. In verses 6-7 Paul suggests some practical ways we should submit to those in authority. What other examples can you think of?

8. In verse 8 Paul says, "Let no debt remain outstanding." Does this mean Christians should never incur any type of debts (mortgage, car and so on)? Explain your answer.

9. Why is love a debt that can never fully be paid (vv. 8-10)?

---

10. In verses 11-14 Paul uses several vivid images to describe "the present time." How does each one give us a picture of how we should (or shouldn't) live?

---

11. Think back over this chapter. In what ways do you need to "put on the Lord Jesus Christ"?

6
To Eat or Not to Eat
Romans 14:1-23

In the late 1800s robed choirs were considered worldly by some Christians. More recently bowling, reading novels and drinking coffee or tea have been severely condemned. Even chewing gum has come under attack!

The Bible contains many clear commands. But it is also silent or ambiguous about many moral issues. These "gray" areas have always been a source of dispute and conflict among Christians, even though the specific areas of dispute change from time to time. What principles should guide us when our actions are criticized by others or when we feel critical toward them? Romans 14 helps us answer these questions.

1. In the 1924 Olympics Eric Liddell refused to run a qualifying race on Sunday, even though failure to qualify would eliminate him from competition. He believed that to run on Sunday would break the commandment, "Remember the Sabbath day by keeping it holy" (Ex 20:8). Do you think his decision was right or wrong? Explain.

2. Read Romans 14. What are some areas of dispute between the "weak" and the "strong" in verses 1-6?

What types of behavior do Christians disagree about today?

3. What attitudes do the weak and the strong tend to have toward each other (vv. 1-4)?

Why might they feel this way?

4. What types of Christians are you most likely to judge or look down on? Why?

5. Why is it wrong to pass judgment on other Christians (vv. 1-13)?

6. When we are *not* around those whose faith is weak, what principles should govern our Christian liberty (vv. 5-23)?

7. When we *are* around those whose faith is weak, what principles should guide our actions, and why (vv. 13-21)?

8. Someone somewhere is bound to be offended by almost anything we do! How can we practically apply these principles?

9. In his treatise *On the Freedom of a Christian Man,* Martin Luther wrote: "A Christian man is a most free lord of all, subject to none. A Christian man is a most dutiful servant of all, subject to all." How do these words summarize the essence of this chapter?

For further thought and prayer: Which of your own practices might distress or destroy another brother or sister in Christ? What practices offend you? Ask God for wisdom to know how to respond in these areas.

7
Unity, Hope and Praise

Romans 15:1-13

Y*ou deserve the best. Look out for number one. Pamper yourself.* These are the watchwords of our age. But in this chapter Paul urges us to stop gazing at our own reflection. For the first time in Romans he holds up the example of Christ, the one who embodies all the qualities God desires in us.

1. When is self-concern appropriate and when does it turn into selfishness?

2. Read Romans 15:1-13. In light of Romans 14, who are the strong and weak Paul mentions in 15:1?

3. What personal attitudes might hinder or help us to bear with the failings of the weak (vv. 1-2)? Explain why.

4. How was Christ (v. 3) the supreme example of what Paul commands in verses 1-2?

5. If we follow Christ's example in this and other areas of our lives, why will we need endurance, encouragement and hope (vv. 4-5)?

Why are Bible study and prayer (vv. 4-5) essential if we are to maintain these attitudes?

6. In contrast to the discord and possible verbal abuse hinted at in Romans 14, what does God desire of us (vv. 5-6)?

7. How can the fact that Christ has accepted us promote both unity and praise (v. 7)?

8. In verses 9-12 Paul quotes from four different Old Testament passages. What words and phrases express the dominant mood of these verses?

Why is this mood appropriate for all who hope in Jesus?

---

9. Paul concludes this passage with a vivid prayer (v. 13). Visualize and describe what is taking place.

---

10. Keeping in mind the context of verses 1-12, how can we become those whose lives overflow with joy, peace and hope (v. 13)?

Spend time praising God for the joy, peace and hope we have in Christ.

8
Brothers and Sisters in Christ

Romans 15:14—16:27

In Christ we have a bond that is stronger than flesh and blood. We are now and will always be brothers and sisters in Christ, members of God's family. This passage introduces us to some of our first-century relatives. As you read about them, notice the care they had for each other.

1. What images come to mind when you think of the first-century church?

2. Read Romans 15:14-33. What do we learn about Paul's apostolic ministry from verses 14-22?

3. What are Paul's immediate and future plans (vv. 23-33)?

4. What do verses 23-33 teach us about relationships among first-century Christians?

5. What impresses you most about their relationships, and why?

6. In what ways can we share material blessings with other Christians?

7. Read Romans 16. In spite of the fact that Paul had never been to Rome, he sends greetings to more than twenty-five people by name. What previous contacts did Paul have with these people (vv. 1-16)?

Why does he appreciate them?

8. Use your imagination. From what we know about Paul and the Romans, how might the people in verses 1-16 have "risked their lives," "worked very hard" and "been a great help" to Paul and others?

In what practical ways might we imitate their example?

9. What type of people were causing divisions and creating problems in the family of God (vv. 17-20)?

How can we overcome the subtle but destructive influence of such people?

10. How do the final words of this letter summarize the scope of our salvation from beginning to end (vv. 25-27)?

9
Review

Romans 9—16

In 1534 William Tyndale wrote this exhortation about *Romans.* "Now go, reader, and follow the order of Paul's writing. First, behold yourself diligently in the law of God, and see there your just condemnation. Second, turn your eyes to Christ, and see in him the great mercy of your very kind and loving Father. Third, remember that Christ did not make atonement that you should anger God again, nor did he cleanse you that you should return (as a swine) to your old puddle again. He wants you to be a new creation and to live a new life, following the will of God and not the sinful nature." Tyndale's words provide a fitting preface to this final study in Romans.

1. Many Christians believe that every unfulfilled promise God made to Israel will be fulfilled to Israel. Others claim that all the promises to Israel are fulfilled in the church. What light does Romans 9—11 shed on this question?

2. In Romans 12—16 Paul discusses several major areas in which our lives are to be living sacrifices to God. What are some of these areas?

3. If we are to be effective servants of God, why is it important that we not think too much or too little of the gifts God has given us?

4. Who are some of the people or institutions that have authority over you?

What practical difference should it make that they have been appointed by God?

5. Imagine that you are in a group of Christians who believe some morally neutral practice (say, drinking milk) is a sign of true spirituality. If you drink milk, you will be accepted. If you don't, you risk being ostracized. What should be your response and why?

6. What types of people in your church or fellowship group tend to be neglected by others?

In what ways might you reach out to such people?

7. In what ways does your church or fellowship group exhibit the qualities of a close-knit family?

8. What can you do to strengthen your relationships with the members of your spiritual family?

9. What is the most important thing you have learned from studying Romans 9—16?

10. What have you enjoyed most about studying the book of Romans?

Leader's Notes

Leading a Bible discussion can be an enjoyable and rewarding experience. But it can also be *scary*—especially if you've never done it before. If this is your feeling, you're in good company. When God asked Moses to lead the Israelites out of Egypt, he replied, "O Lord, please send someone else to do it!" (Ex 4:13).

When Solomon became king of Israel, he felt the task was far beyond his abilities. "I am only a little child and do not know how to carry out my duties. . . . Who is able to govern this great people of yours?" (1 Kings 3:7, 9).

When God called Jeremiah to be a prophet, he replied, "Ah, Sovereign LORD, . . . I do not know how to speak; I am only a child" (Jer 1:6).

The list goes on. The apostles were "unschooled, ordinary men" (Acts 4:13). Timothy was young, frail and frightened. Paul's "thorn in the flesh" made him feel weak. But God's response to all of his servants—including you—is essentially the same: "My grace is sufficient for you" (2 Cor 12:9). Relax. God helped these people in spite of their weaknesses, and he can help you in spite of your feelings of inadequacy.

There is another reason why you should feel encouraged. Leading a Bible discussion is not difficult if you follow certain guidelines. You don't need to be an expert on the Bible or a trained teacher. The suggestions listed below should enable you to effectively and enjoyably fulfill your role as leader.

Preparing to Lead

1. Ask God to help you understand and apply the passage to your own life. Unless this happens, you will not be prepared to lead others. Pray too for the various members of the group. Ask God to give you an enjoyable and profitable time together studying his Word.

2. As you begin each study, read and reread the assigned Bible passage to familiarize yourself with what the author is saying. In the case of book studies, you may want to read through the entire book prior to the first study. This will give you a helpful overview of its contents.

3. This study guide is based on the New International Version of the Bible. It will help you and the group if you use this translation as the basis for your study and discussion. Encourage others to use the NIV also, but allow them the freedom to use whatever translation they prefer.

4. Carefully work through each question in the study. Spend time in meditation and reflection as you formulate your answers.

5. Write your answers in the space provided in the study guide. This will help you to express your understanding of the passage clearly.

6. It might help you to have a Bible dictionary handy. Use it to look up any unfamiliar words, names or places. (For additional help on how to study a passage, see chapter five of *Leading Bible Discussions,* IVP.)

7. Once you have finished your own study of the passage, familiarize yourself with the leader's notes for the study you are leading. These are designed to help you in several ways. First, they tell you the purpose the study guide author had in mind while writing the study. Take time to think through how the study questions work together to accomplish that purpose. Second, the notes provide you with additional background information or comments on some of the questions. This information can be useful if people have difficulty understanding or answering a question. Third, the leader's notes can alert you to potential problems you may encounter during the study.

8. If you wish to remind yourself of anything mentioned in the leader's notes, make a note to yourself below that question in the study.

Leading the Study

1. Begin the study on time. Unless you are leading an evangelistic Bible study, open with prayer, asking God to help you to understand and apply the passage.

2. Be sure that everyone in your group has a study guide. Encourage them to prepare beforehand for each discussion by working through the questions in the guide.

3. At the beginning of your first time together, explain that these studies are meant to be discussions not lectures. Encourage the members of the group to participate. However, do not put pressure on those who may be hesitant to speak during the first few sessions.

4. Read the introductory paragraph at the beginning of the discussion. This will orient the group to the passage being studied.

5. Read the passage aloud if you are studying one chapter or less. You may choose to do this yourself, or someone else may read if he or she has been asked to do so prior to the study. Longer passages may occasionally be read in parts at different times during the study. Some studies may cover several chapters. In such cases reading aloud would probably take too much time, so the group members should simply read the assigned passages prior to the study.

6. As you begin to ask the questions in the guide, keep several things in mind. First, the questions are designed to be used just as they are written. If you wish, you may simply read them aloud to the group. Or you may prefer to express them in your own words. However, unnecessary rewording of the questions is not recommended.

Second, the questions are intended to guide the group toward understanding and applying the *main idea* of the passage. The author of the guide has stated his or her view of this central idea in the *purpose* of the study in the leader's notes. You should try to understand how the passage expresses this idea and how the study questions work together to lead the group in that direction.

There may be times when it is appropriate to deviate from the study guide. For example, a question may have already been answered. If so, move on to the next question. Or someone may raise an important question not covered in the guide. Take time to discuss it! The important thing is to use discretion. There may be many routes you can travel to reach the goal of the study. But the easiest route is usually the one the author has suggested.

7. Avoid answering your own questions. If necessary, repeat or rephrase them until they are clearly understood. An eager group quickly becomes passive and silent if they think the leader will do most of the talking.

8. Don't be afraid of silence. People may need time to think about the question before formulating their answers.

9. Don't be content with just one answer. Ask, "What do the rest of you think?" or "Anything else?" until several people have given answers to the question.

10. Acknowledge all contributions. Try to be affirming whenever possible. Never reject an answer. If it is clearly wrong, ask, "Which verse led you to that conclusion?" or again, "What do the rest of you think?"

11. Don't expect every answer to be addressed to you, even though this will probably happen at first. As group members become more at ease, they will begin to truly interact with each other. This is one sign of a healthy discussion.

12. Don't be afraid of controversy. It can be very stimulating. If you don't resolve an issue completely, don't be frustrated. Move on and keep it in mind for later. A subsequent study may solve the problem.

13. Stick to the passage under consideration. It should be the source for answering the questions. Discourage the group from unnecessary cross-referencing. Likewise, stick to the subject and avoid going off on tangents.

14. Periodically summarize what the *group* has said about the passage. This helps to draw together the various ideas mentioned and gives continuity to the study. But don't preach.

15. Conclude your time together with conversational prayer. Be sure to ask God's help to apply those things which you learned in the study.

16. End on time.

Many more suggestions and helps are found in *Leading Bible Discussions* (IVP). Reading and studying through that would be well worth your time.

Components of Small Groups

A healthy small group should do more than study the Bible. There are four components you should consider as you structure your time together.

Nurture. Being a part of a small group should be a nurturing and edifying experience. You should grow in your knowledge and love of God and each other. If we are to properly love God, we must know and keep his commandments (Jn 14:15). That is why Bible study should be a foundational part of your small group. But you can be nurtured by other things as well. You can memorize Scripture, read and discuss a book, or occasionally listen to a tape of a good speaker.

Community. Most people have a need for close friendships. Your small group can be an excellent place to cultivate such relationships. Allow time for informal interaction before and after the study. Have a time of sharing during the meeting. Do fun things together as a group, such as a potluck supper or a picnic. Have someone bring refreshments to the meeting. Be creative!

Worship. A portion of your time together can be spent in worship and prayer. Praise God together for who he is. Thank him for what he has done and is doing in your lives and in the world. Pray for each other's needs. Ask God to help you to apply what you have learned. Sing hymns together.

Mission. Many small groups decide to work together in some form of outreach. This can be a practical way of applying what you have learned. You can host a series of evangelistic discussions for your friends or neighbors. You can visit people at a home for the elderly. Help a widow with cleaning or repair jobs around her home. Such projects can have a transforming influence on your group.

For a detailed discussion of the nature and function of small groups, read *Small Group Leaders' Handbook* or *Good Things Come in Small Groups* (both from IVP).

Part 1. A New Life. Romans 1—8.
Study 1. Good News from God. Romans 1:1-17.

Purpose: This study introduces us to Paul, the Romans and the gospel which united and transformed them. We also begin to catch some of Paul's enthusiasm for the gospel.

Question 1. Almost every study begins with an "approach" question, which is meant to be asked *before* the passage is read. These questions are important for several reasons.

First, they help the group to warm up to each other. No matter how well a group may know each other or how comfortable they may be with each other, there is always a stiffness that needs to be overcome before people will begin to talk openly. A good question will break the ice.

Second, approach questions get people thinking along the lines of the topic of the study. Most people will have lots of different things going on in their minds (dinner, an important meeting coming up, how to get the car fixed) that will have nothing to do with the study. A creative question will get their attention and draw them into the discussion.

Third, approach questions can reveal where our thoughts or feelings need to be transformed by Scripture. This is why it is especially important *not* to read the passage before the approach question is asked. The passage will tend to color the honest reactions people would otherwise give because they are of course *supposed* to think the way the Bible does. Giving honest responses to various issues before they find out what the Bible says may help them to see where their thoughts or attitudes need to be changed.

Question 3. These verses are packed with information. Paul touches on the gospel's origin ("of God" v. 1), its attestation (v. 2), its substance (vv. 3-4), its scope (v. 5), its purpose and its goal (v. 5). But don't spend too much time on these verses; the ideas are elaborated elsewhere in Romans.

Question 9. Luther came to this conclusion during the period between November 1515 and September 1516 while expounding the letter to the Romans to his students at Wittenberg University. It was the initial spark which ignited the Protestant Reformation.

Once again, many of the ideas in verse 17—such as the gospel, righteousness and faith—will be covered later in Romans. However, if people are confused about the meaning of righteousness, you might read the following definition. "Righteousness from God has two aspects: legal and moral. Legally, God accepts us as though we had fulfilled every obligation of the law. Morally, God transforms us so that we can fulfill his law." Legal righteousness is described in chapters 1—5. Moral righteousness is described in chapters 6—8 (as well as 12—16).

Study 2. The Wrath of God. Romans 1:18-32.

Purpose: To understand the downward spiral of humanity and how our rebellion evokes the wrath of God. This study and the next two help us grasp why people need the gospel.

Question 3. Psalm 19 describes the language and testimony of creation more fully than Romans 1:19-20. You might ask someone in the group to read aloud verses 1-6 of this psalm.

Question 5. If you look closely, you will notice several levels: idolatry (vv. 21-23), impurity (vv. 24-25), perversion (vv. 26-27), depravity (vv. 28-31) and a flagrant disregard of God's judgment (v. 32). Of course there are many ways of describing each level of descent. Let the group come up with their own descriptions.

Paul is not claiming that every non-Christian exhibits all of these characteristics to the same degree. But they have characterized humanity ever since the fall of Adam and Eve.

Question 6. You might add interest by bringing a newspaper to the study. Give each person in the group a page from the paper, then ask the group to answer this question with illustrations from current news items. (Of course, they don't need to restrict their answers to the newspaper.) If you decide to do this exercise, keep track of time so the group can fully answer the remaining questions.

Study 3. The Judgment of God. Romans 2:1-29.

Purpose: To understand the principles by which God will judge the world. This will help us grasp why even "respectable" or religious people need the gospel.

Question 2. As the group reads this chapter, ask them to notice how frequently Paul refers to our *deeds* and to the *law*.

In this chapter Paul uses a technique known as *diatribe*. He debates with an imaginary opponent in order to teach principles of divine judgment. We

must keep in mind, therefore, that he is not accusing the Romans of being judgmental. Rather they are "overhearing" Paul's conversation with a self-righteous, judgmental person. Paul wants the Romans to realize why all non-Christians are under God's judgment—even those who are very religious.
Question 3. If the discussion of question 2 covers this question, skip it.
Questions 4-5. In verses 5-16 Paul states that God will decide our eternal destiny on the basis of our obedience or disobedience. He is not suggesting, however, that anyone *will* be saved by their obedience. God's verdict is not discussed until the next study. So if this issue arises in your group, you may want to suggest that people wait till study four to discuss it.
Question 9. Encourage members of your group to speak the truth in love. This question should not be a springboard for condemning others—especially in a chapter which warns us against being judgmental.
Questions 10-11. Throughout verses 17-29 Paul exposes the danger of re-lying on external factors (being Jewish, knowing the law, being circumcised) rather than internal spiritual reality. Likewise, many people today assume that because they go to church, have been baptized or confirmed, or read their Bible regularly, they are exempt from God's judgment. Paul will go on to argue (Rom 3:21-31) that only faith in Jesus Christ delivers us from God's judgment.

Study 4. The Verdict. Romans 3:1-20.

Purpose: To consider the verdict which Paul, Scripture and God agree the whole world deserves.
Question 2. Encourage the group to think of more advantages than Paul mentions.
Question 3. If these questions don't bring out adequate discussion of the passage, you could reword them, such as, "If our unrighteousness brings out God's righteousness and increases his glory, then why is he condemning us?"
Question 5. In verses 10-18 Paul quotes from Psalms 14:1-3; 53:1-3; Eccle-siastes 7:20; Psalms 5:9; 140:3; 10:7; Isaiah 59:7-8 and Psalm 36:1.
Question 7. This is a difficult question. Paul has been describing the con-dition of humanity prior to God's saving grace in Christ, the subject of the next study. Whenever God's grace is extended to a person, he or she is always in the helpless and condemned state which Paul has described. Therefore, if a person is truly seeking God, we can conclude that God's grace is active in softening the person's fallen and rebellious heart.
Question 8. This is an important question for drawing together and sum-marizing what Paul has emphasized in the first two and a half chapters.

Question 10. Until this fact sinks in, we will never appreciate the magnitude of God's grace.

Study 5. The Righteousness from God. Romans 3:21-31.

Purpose: This study considers how God can be just and yet justify those who deserve his wrath. This will help us appreciate what Jesus has done for us on the cross.

Question 2. Righteousness from God is through faith and is freely given by his grace (that is, undeservedly). Righteousness by law, according to Romans 2, was possible only by fully obeying the law and thus deserving God's favor—something Paul claims no one has ever done.

Question 7. The words *sacrifice of atonement* are an attempt to simplify the Greek word normally translated as "propitiation."

In the phrase "faith in his blood," (v. 25) the word *blood* refers to Christ's death.

Some people claim the idea that God's wrath must be appeased through a human sacrifice is pagan, barbaric, unworthy of God. We must realize, however, that God not only demanded the sacrifice but *became* the sacrifice through the Incarnation. This is certainly not a pagan act—it demonstrates the magnitude of God's justice, love and grace.

Questions 11-12. Meditating on the cross should fill us with praise and thanks to the God who loves us and gave his only Son for us. This, in turn, should have a profound effect on our attitude toward sin, as Paul will emphasize later.

Study 6. The Example of Abraham. Romans 4:1-25.

Purpose: To consider why Abraham is a timeless example of hope in the midst of a hopeless situation.

Question 2. It is not surprising that Paul chose Abraham as his primary example. Abraham was the patriarch of the Jewish people and was greatly revered. In this chapter Paul challenges the commonly held assumption that Abraham had merited God's favor because of his obedience.

Abraham also represents someone who lived before the Law was given and who was declared righteous while uncircumcised. David, on the other hand, was circumcised and lived after the Law had been given. Yet Abraham and David did not hope in themselves but testify to being declared righteous by faith.

Question 5. Circumcision was a sign of the covenant between God and Abraham's descendants (see Gen 17). Anyone who was uncircumcised was cut off from the covenant (Gen 17:14). The Jews of Paul's day assumed, therefore, that circumcision was necessary if one wanted to partake of the blessings of the covenant, including salvation. Those outside the covenant were without hope. Paul points out that Abraham was declared righteous *before* he was circumcised.

Question 8. Abraham's body was "as good as dead," but the God of resurrection gave him and Sarah life. They had no child nor the ability to conceive one, but the God of creation gave them that ability.

Question 9. Encourage people to look for parallels between Abraham's experience and our own. For example, he wanted a child, but he was too old and, as one person has said, "Sarah's womb was a tomb." Likewise, we desire to be accepted by God, but we are spiritually dead and have no hope of living up to God's standards. But both to Abraham and us God's promises offer hope in a hopeless situation.

Question 11. Hope is not the same as wishful thinking—"I hope this will happen." Notice that Abraham's hope was a trust that "God had power to do what he had promised" (v. 21). Our hope should be anchored both in the character and promises of God. Likewise, faith and hope are demonstrated externally. They do not remain merely internal.

Study 7. Reasons to Rejoice. Romans 5:1-21.

Purpose: To consider why we have several firm and lasting reasons to rejoice in Christ.

Question 4. Concerning the word *glory,* John Stott writes: "But what is 'the glory of God'? . . . The glory of God is the manifestation of God, his radiant splendor, the outward shining of his inward being. And already his glory has been partly revealed—in the universe, in human beings and supremely in Jesus Christ. . . . One day, however, the glory of God will be fully revealed, and 'we exult in hope' of this prospect" (*Believing and Obeying Jesus Christ* [Downers Grove, Ill.: InterVarsity Press, 1980], p. 95).

Questions 5-6. Encourage the group to explore how their attitudes toward suffering can become more biblical. We are to *rejoice* in suffering—not because we are masochists who enjoy pain, but because God uses suffering to transform our character. Yet how often do we rejoice in trials and difficulties?

Question 7. It is difficult to see the connection between "hope does not disappoint us" (v. 5) and "because God has poured out his love into our hearts (v. 5)." How can a past experience affect a future hope? The answer is that we know our hope will not disappoint us because God loves us. And we know God loves us because we have experienced his love through the

Holy Spirit and the death of Christ.

Questions 10-11. Many people find it difficult to believe in a literal, historical Adam and Eve. Yet there is no question that Paul (and hence Scripture) believed they were real persons. According to these verses, Adam and the consequences of his disobedience are just as real as Christ and the results of his obedience. In fact, without the former, the work of Christ makes little sense at all.

Study 8. New Life, New Lifestyle. Romans 6:1—7:6.

Purpose: To realize that our new life in Christ demands a new lifestyle.

Question 2. Some members of your group may be perplexed over Paul's close association of baptism and conversion. It is clear from chapter 4 that Paul understood the difference between a sign and what it signified. Yet in the early church, baptism was the visible and public sign that a person accepted Christ as his or her Savior. It was the event that outwardly marked one's acceptance into the church.

Question 3. Instead of the phrase *rendered powerless* in verse 6, some translations have the word *destroyed.* The former captures Paul's meaning best. Anyone in your group could testify to the presence of sin in our lives. But sin is no longer our master.

Question 6. The idea of counting or reckoning (KJV) ourselves dead to sin has been much abused. It is often presented as something we must do in order to break sin's mastery over us. But Paul wants us to realize that sin's power over us has *already* been broken by Christ. We are to live in light of that fact.

Question 7. This is a very important question. Our success in ridding our lives of sinful behavior often depends on putting righteous behavior in its place.

Question 8. Throughout verses 15-23 Paul assumes that every Christian is a slave of righteousness. Notice his language: "You used to be slaves to sin. . . . You have been set free from sin and have become slaves to righteousness." He is not suggesting that when we sin, we cease to be slaves of righteousness and become slaves of sin. Rather, sin is inappropriate because we *are* slaves of righteousness.

Question 10. In Paul's illustration (7:1-3) the woman was bound by law to her husband. She was married to her husband, not to the law. But who was our former spouse according to verses 4-6? The law? Or were we bound *by* law to sin? Commentators differ on this question. It might be interesting to find out what the group thinks (but don't take too much time on this).

Study 9. Our Struggle with Sin. Romans 7:7-25.
Purpose: To realize that sin, not the law (which is good), was responsible for
enslaving and killing us, and that only Christ can deliver us from sin's power.
Question 3. Paul makes two surprising statements about himself, the law
and sin. One is, "For apart from law, sin is dead" (v. 8). This does not mean
that sin, apart from the law, ceases to exist or to enslave us. But rather, "sin
is not taken into account when there is no law" (Rom 5:13). Apart from the
law the evil nature of sin is not revealed. When the law comes, however, sin
"springs to life" (v. 9) because certain actions and attitudes are now identified
as *sin.*
   The other statement is, "I was alive apart from law" (v. 9). Paul is not
speaking absolutely, but rather of his legal status prior to the law. He, like
everyone else since Adam and Eve, was spiritually dead before believing in
Christ. But the death sentence was not legally passed until "the commandment came, sin sprang to life and I died" (v. 9).
Questions 5-7. Verses 13-25 have been the subject of much controversy. Do
they describe Paul's experience before or after his conversion? Or is he not
speaking about himself in particular at all, but rather about humanity in
general?
   It would probably be best not to discuss this question unless someone in
the group raises it. If that happens, however, you might simply ask the group
members to briefly give their opinion and then move on to the next question.
The issue is important, but it is very difficult to resolve in a brief amount of
time.
   If the discussion persists, you might offer this suggestion. Many commentators point out that Paul uses the past tense in verses 7-13, while describing
what most would agree is his preconversion experience. But in verses 14-25
he suddenly shifts to the present tense. One possible explanation is that he
begins at that point to discuss his *Christian* experience.
   On the other hand, this view assumes that a new subject is introduced in
verses 14-25. Yet these verses seem to be an elaboration of verse 13, which
describes how the law brought about Paul's spiritual death as a *non-Christian.*
What is the solution? Let the group decide!
Questions 8-9. Those who believe verses 14-25 describe Paul's Christian
experience point out how closely his struggles resemble our own as Christians. But even though the *struggles* are similar, the *outcome* of these struggles
seems to be very different from what Paul has taught us to expect (see Rom
6). For example, Paul states that in his mind he is "a slave to God's law" (v.
25). Yet he is unable to *obey* God's law and is an unwilling prisoner and slave

to sin (vv. 14, 23, 25). He is comparable to a prisoner in a POW camp. In his heart and mind he is totally loyal to his country, but in reality he is a prisoner of those he opposes. Encourage your group to consider not only whether we struggle with sin in a manner similar to Paul, but also whether we are still prisoners and slaves to sin. This will be discussed further in the next study.

Question 10. Our desire to be rescued from "this body of death" (v. 24) will only be ultimately realized when we are resurrected (see 8:23). But chapter 8 tells us that Christ has already rescued us from the penalty and power of sin (see 8:1-14).

Question 11. In Romans 1—5 Paul argued that only Christ can deliver us from the penalty of sin. In 6—8 he argues that only Christ can deliver us from the power of sin.

Study 10. The Spirit Brings Life. Romans 8:1-17.

Purpose: To realize that the Spirit brings life instead of death, peace instead of anxiety, and power to obey God instead of sin.

Questions 2-3. It is important to see the relationship between chapters 7 and 8. In chapter 7 Paul described two "laws" (principles) which were at war with each other: the law of his mind (which delighted in God's law) and the law of sin (vv. 21-23). As long as the battle only included these two laws, Paul was a prisoner of the law of sin (v. 23). The result, therefore, was death (v. 24). But in chapter 8 a new "law" is introduced: the law of the Spirit (v. 2). When we became Christians, he set us free from the law of sin and death.

Question 4. It is often claimed that Paul is contrasting two categories of *Christian* experience in verses 5-8. We have one type of experience if we live according to the sinful nature and an entirely different experience if we live according to the Spirit.

But this idea is based on a misreading of the passage. According to verse 4, Christians do *not* live according to the sinful nature but according to the Spirit. This is reiterated in verse 9, where it is made clear that Paul is contrasting Christian and non-Christian experience. John Stott comments: "Here, then, are two categories of people (those who are in the flesh, and those who are in the Spirit), who have two mentalities (called the mind of the flesh and the mind of the Spirit), which lead to two patterns of conduct (walking according to the flesh and walking according to the Spirit), and result in two spiritual states (death and life)" (John Stott, *Men Made New* [Downers Grove, Ill.: InterVarsity Press, 1966], pp. 87-88).

The word *controlled* (v. 9) is not found in the Greek text, which is better captured here by the RSV: "But you are not in the flesh, you are in the Spirit, if in fact the Spirit of God dwells in you."

Questions 8-9. Paul's statements must be considered in context. He is not saying, "Obey the Spirit and you will live; disobey the Spirit and you will die." Living according to the Spirit includes all that Paul has described previously: trusting in the sin offering of God's Son (v. 3), belonging to Christ (v. 9), having the Spirit live in us (v. 9), setting our minds on what the Spirit desires (v. 5) and submitting to God's law (v. 7). These are the characteristics of God's sons (v. 14). Likewise, living according to the sinful nature is viewed as the antithesis of each of these aspects of living according to the Spirit. Those who live according to the sinful nature do not trust in Christ or his Spirit.

It should be noted that the NIV blurs some of the subtle distinctions Paul makes in verses 4-13. In verse 4, *live according to the Spirit* is literally "*walk* according to the spirit.*" This verse looks at our *conduct.* In verse 5 the phrase *live in accordance with the Spirit* is literally "*are* according to the Spirit." It looks at who we are in relation to the Spirit: those he lives in as opposed to those who do not have the Spirit. The NASB and RSV give a more accurate translation of these verses. Verse 13 (clearly translated in the NIV) focuses on the fact that the Spirit is our source of *life.*

Question 10. People naturally assume that the leading of the Spirit has to do with guidance. However, here and in Galatians 5:18 the context implies that the Spirit's leading relates to *holiness.* He leads God's children to become more like Christ.

Question 11. Notice the balance between our responsibility and the Spirit's. *We* are to put to death the misdeeds of the body *by the Spirit.*

Study 11. Glorious Conquerors. Romans 8:18-39.
Purpose: To realize that our present sufferings cannot compare with the future glory we will receive in Christ.

Question 2. Some Christians believe the normal Christian life is meant to be free from sickness, suffering and difficulty. They claim that if we are not healthy, wealthy and happy, it is because of personal sin or unbelief. This passage (including v. 17) provides a powerful corrective to this kind of thinking. We are glorious conquerors not because our lives are free from suffering but because we triumph in spite of our suffering.

These verses also describe the glories of the future, but these will be discussed later in the study.

Question 7. In order to understand this verse we must understand Paul's definition of *good.* Obviously from the context it cannot mean freedom from suffering, hardship or difficulties. God's good purpose is that we become "conformed to the likeness of his Son" (vv. 28-29).

Question 8. Because of words such as *foreknew* and *predestined,* this question might generate controversy. It would be impossible, however, from this one passage to solve all the problems related to God's sovereignty and human responsibility. It is much more important for the group to see that from beginning to end God is working to accomplish his purposes for us.

Although our glorification is still future, Paul speaks of it in the past tense to indicate its certainty.

Question 10. It is true that Paul states: "Who will bring any charge against those whom God has chosen?" (v. 33). Yet Satan, others and even our own consciences often accuse us and attempt to make us feel unworthy of God's love. Paul's point is that such charges cannot be upheld, not that they do not exist.

Question 12. These verses are full of encouragement, beauty and hope. Be sure to leave enough time to discuss them!

Study 12. Review. Romans 1—8.

Purpose: To review both the meaning and significance of Romans 1—8.

The first eight chapters of Romans contain enough material for a lifetime of thought and reflection. This study only attempts to review and apply the major themes of these chapters.

Questions 1-2. If we were not tempted to be ashamed of Christ and the gospel, then Christ would not have warned us about this temptation (Mk 8:38).

Question 8. At the conclusion of this question, you might encourage the group to continue their study of Romans. Part 2 of this guide covers chapters 9—16. It is unfortunate how many people never get beyond the first eight chapters!

Part 2. A New Lifestyle. Romans 9—16.
Study 1. The Potter and His Clay. Romans 9:1-29.

Purpose: To explore the subject of Israel's unbelief from the standpoint of God's sovereignty.

Question 3. In verses 6-13 Paul develops the idea of an Israel within Israel. Abraham had two sons: Ishmael and Isaac, but only Isaac was chosen to carry on the lineage leading eventually to the nation of Israel. Likewise, Isaac had two sons: Jacob and Esau, but only Jacob's descendants are considered Israelites and thus heirs of the covenant God made with Abraham. Paul's point is that God has always chosen to fulfill his promises to some, not all, of Abraham's descendants. But he has never failed to fulfill his promises to those he has chosen.

The statement "Jacob I loved, but Esau I hated" (v. 13) may trouble some of the members of your group. After all, doesn't God love everyone? The quote is from Malachi 1:2-3, where the context describes God's treatment of Esau's descendants, the Edomites, as opposed to his treatment of Jacob's descendants, the Israelites. The contrast is so great that it is like the difference between love and hate.

Question 4. The subject of election never fails to stir up controversy, but it is difficult to avoid in this chapter. This question is designed to allow people to vent their feelings, positive or negative, about this subject. The next question will ask them to wrestle with whether it is just or unjust for God to choose some and not others.

Questions 6-7. Paul never gives a direct answer to the question raised in verse 19 because those who ask it presume to sit in judgment on God. In effect Paul says, "Who do you think you are? God can do whatever he wants with his own creation!" Nevertheless, in light of the universal guilt of humanity it is amazing that God has chosen *anyone* when he would be perfectly just to condemn us all.

Question 8. In verses 25-26 Paul quotes from Hosea, whose wife (symbolic of Israel) broke her marriage vows through unfaithfulness. Nevertheless, she (and Israel) would one day be restored to her husband. Paul sees this as an illustration of how God's grace has been extended not only to unfaithful Jews but also to Gentiles.

In verses 27-29 Paul quotes from Isaiah, who warned that God's judgment through the Assyrians would only leave a remnant who would return from exile. Paul sees this as an illustration of the remnant of believing Jews in his day. Although they were few in number, at least some believed!

Study 2. Misguided Zeal. Romans 9:30—10:21.
Purpose: To consider Israel's unbelief from the standpoint of human responsibility.

Question 3. If necessary, *briefly* summarize Romans 3:10-18.

Question 5. The original wording of Deuteronomy 30:11-14 describes the righteousness that is by law. Paul's change of wording highlights the differences between these two ways of seeking salvation.

Question 6. The confession "Jesus is Lord" was one of the earliest Christian creeds (see 1 Cor 12:3). It briefly summarized who Jesus is and the position to which he had been exalted following his incarnation, death, burial and resurrection.

Question 9. These verses underscore the fact that God has chosen to communicate the gospel through people. When we presume he will save those who have never heard the gospel, we turn our backs on the responsibility he has given us!

Study 3. The Future of Israel. Romans 11:1-36.

Purpose: To realize that Israel's unbelief is partial, purposeful and temporary.

Question 6. Verse 22 might be disturbing to some of the members of your group because it seems to imply that we can lose our salvation. But Paul is not talking about individual Gentiles but rather Gentiles as a group. They have become partakers of Israel's blessings because of Jewish unbelief. They can just as easily lose these blessings (as a group) if they fail to believe in Christ. In other words, their privileged status is due to *faith* not the fact that they are Gentiles.

Question 7. Dispensational and Reformed theologians differ in their understanding of the relationship between Israel and the church. The former believe that God has two separate programs in history: one for Israel and one for the church, and that the two groups are totally unrelated. Reformed theologians believe that the promises to Israel have been (or will be) fulfilled in the church, and that God no longer has a special relationship with the nation of Israel. This passage seems to stress both the continuity between Israel and the church, and the fact that God has not rejected his people. Is this dispensational, Reformed or neither? You decide!

Question 8. In verse 26 Paul states, "And so all Israel will be saved." Not all interpreters agree on the meaning of "all Israel." Calvin, for example, thought that it referred to all of the redeemed, both Jews and Gentiles. If this is so, then Paul is simply saying that when the full number of people are saved, then "all Israel" will be saved—because the two are synonymous! This interpretation, however, overlooks the fact that in this chapter and elsewhere Paul speaks of Israel and the Gentiles as two distinct groups. The former have experienced hardening *until* the full number of Gentiles have been saved. Then Israel will turn from their unbelief and be saved. In other words, this passage leads us to expect that Israel as a group (but not necessarily every individual) will one day experience corporate repentance. When will this occur? Verse 26 seems to indicate that it will be at the Second Coming of Christ.

Study 4. Living Sacrifices. Romans 12:1-21.

Purpose: To begin to consider our proper response to God's mercy and grace.
Question 2. God's grace and mercy provide the proper motivation for godly living. We need to be filled with a sense of his mercy toward us in Christ before we can respond in the manner described in Romans 12—16. This question can be a reminder of all that we are and have in Christ.

Question 5. The Greek word translated "transformed" (*metamorphos,* v. 2) is the word from which we get *metamorphosis.* God is changing us from spiritual caterpillars into butterflies!

Question 6. Notice that a sacrificial life is not only pleasing to God (v. 1), it is pleasing to us (v. 2)!

Question 8. Paul does not intend for this to be a complete list of spiritual gifts. Other gifts are mentioned in 1 Corinthians 12, Ephesians 4 and 1 Peter 4.

Question 10. Chances are that someone in your group will ask the meaning of "heap burning coals on his head" (v. 20). F. F. Bruce offers this paraphrase and explanation: " 'Treat your enemy kindly, for this may make him ashamed and lead to his repentance.' In other words, the best way to get rid of an enemy is to turn him into a friend, and so 'overcome evil with good' (verse 21)" (*Romans,* p. 230).

Study 5. Submitting to Authorities. Romans 13:1-14.

Purpose: To consider why it is appropriate for Christians to submit to those in positions of authority.

Question 3. Paul is not simply discussing authority in the abstract, but rather speaks concretely of "the authorities that exist" (v. 1). Those in positions of authority "derive their origin, right, and power from God" (John Murray, *The Epistle to the Romans* [Grand Rapids, Mich.: Eerdmans, 1968], p. 148).

Question 6. Acts 4:19-20 provide a scriptural basis for civil disobedience when obedience to God would be compromised or excluded by obedience to those in authority. In such cases those in authority have gone beyond the limits of the authority given to them by God.

Question 10. Encourage the group first to visualize the images Paul has in mind before trying to interpret the meaning of these images (day = the Second Coming of Christ and so on). This is always a good practice when dealing with biblical imagery.

Study 6. To Eat or Not to Eat. Romans 14:1-23.

Purpose: To consider what principles should guide us in areas where Christians disagree over what is right and wrong.

Question 2. This is a study in which you need to be especially sensitive to the members of your group. Some of them may disagree about whether certain practices are right or wrong. This study is not designed to make everyone agree with everyone else, but to enable us to accept and love those with whom we *disagree*.

Question 6. We must be careful to understand what Paul means by "weak" faith. In this context he does not mean a weak trust in God but rather an incomplete or inaccurate understanding of the Christian life. Likewise in verse 23 Paul states that "everything that does not come from faith is sin." The "faith" he refers to is the conviction that our actions can be done with a clear conscience.

Question 8. Paul is certainly not telling us to give up every practice which is disapproved of by another Christian. There wouldn't be much left for us to do! On the other hand, some interpreters claim that we are only to abstain from an activity if it causes someone else to sin. But what if our actions alienate us from another brother or sister and so threaten the peace and joy that is to characterize our fellowship? Should we abstain simply to maintain peace and harmony with that person? Try to clarify some of these issues as your group discusses this question.

For further thought and prayer: Some groups might feel uncomfortable discussing these questions publicly. For example, someone in the group might feel that drinking is not a sin. Someone else might think it is. The former might not wish to reveal what he or she does privately. However, if your group would feel comfortable discussing these questions, then ask them before question 9. But be careful not to let the study go too long!

Study 7. Unity, Hope and Praise. Romans 15:1-13.

Purpose: To consider how following Christ's example can bring unity, hope and praise.

Question 2. Verses 1-6 are a continuation of Paul's discussion in chapter 14. It is important, therefore, to interpret the words *strong* and *weak* in light of that context.

Question 5. Endurance and encouragement come from the Scriptures (v. 4) and they come from God (v. 5), the Author of Scripture.

Question 6. Paul underscores the fact that we are one in Christ in spite of our differences. It is important that we exhibit that unity in our fellowship and worship.

Question 7. Verse 7 begins a transition in Paul's discussion. In verse 6 he spoke of the fact that our unity should culminate in praise to God. When this occurs, we fulfill those Old Testament Scriptures which foretold that the Gentiles would one day praise God and put their hope in him for salvation (vv. 7-13). Because Paul is the apostle to the Gentiles (vv. 14-22), he is especially eager to see the Gentiles in Rome (and elsewhere) fulfill their calling.

Question 9. Paul pictures us as a vessel into which God pours joy and peace. These qualities are poured out so abundantly on us and in us that we begin to overflow with hope. This is very visual imagery, so it is best to try and picture what is taking place before you try to fully understand Paul's meaning.

Study 8. Brothers and Sisters in Christ. Romans 15:14—16:27.
Purpose: To observe how first-century Christians can be an example to us of love and mutual service.

Question 4. In verses 25-28 Paul mentions "a contribution for the poor among the saints in Jerusalem." This gift to the poor is also discussed in 1 Corinthians 16:1-4 and 2 Corinthians 8—9. In addition to being an act of love, it helped to strengthen the bond between the Jews in Jerusalem and the Gentiles converted under Paul's ministry. It was during Paul's visit to Jerusalem that he was arrested (Acts 21). He did later make it to Rome, as he had hoped, but only under guard (Acts 28).

Question 7. In 16:1-2 Paul commends to the Romans a woman named Phoebe, a "servant" of the church in Cenchrea. Cenchrea was one of the two seaports of Corinth, the city from which Paul was writing this letter. It may be that Phoebe carried the letter to the Romans.

The word *servant* (diakanos), which is used in reference to Phoebe can mean either "servant" or "deacon." Since both meanings are possible, we cannot say with certainty which meaning Paul had in mind. Some people object to the idea that a woman could hold the office of deacon in the church. Yet F. F. Bruce writes: "That the duties of a *diakonos* could be performed by either men or women is suggested by I Timothy iii. II, where "their wives" (AV, NEV) is more probably to be rendered "women" (RV), i.e. "women-deacons" (*Romans,* p. 270).

In verse 7 Paul greets Andronicus and Junias, referring to them as "outstanding among the apostles." The word *apostle* had a broad and narrower meaning. Broadly speaking, it simply referred to "one who is sent." In a Christian context it could mean "one who is sent by Christ to proclaim the gospel." There were certain men, however, including Paul, who were appointed by

Christ to the *office* of apostle. Thus the word took on a narrower, technical meaning. Andronicus and Junias were undoubtedly "apostles" in the broader sense, equivalent today to what we would call "missionaries."

Question 9. In verses 17-20 Paul gives the first clear indication of a serious threat to the Romans. His description of these people indicates that they had libertarian tendencies (v. 18). And although they probably claimed to be Christians, these troublemakers were really servants of Satan (v. 20). Paul is confident, however, that the Romans will not succumb to their deception (v. 20).

Study 9. Review. Romans 9—16.

Purpose: To reflect on some of the important issues raised in Romans 9—16 and to reconsider how they should affect our lives.

Question 1. This question is designed to cause the group to think about Paul's concerns in Romans 9—11 from a slightly different perspective. Paul wondered whether God had rejected his people, whether his promises to them had failed. The answer depends on how one defines *his people* or *Israel.* Do these words now apply only to the church and not to ethnic Israel, or does God still have a special relationship with ethnic Israel?

Question 10. Every other question in this study deals with Romans 9—16, but this one gives the group a chance to reflect on their overall experience of *Romans.*

Since this is the final study in Romans, the group needs to begin thinking about what they would like to study next. Perhaps you might have an informal time of fellowship at your next meeting and decide what to study then. Bring several study guides with you so the group can become familiar with the options available.

Jack Kuhatschek, a former staff member with Inter-Varsity Christian Fellowship, is Bible study editor for InterVarsity Press. He is the author of How to Study the Bible *and the LifeBuilder Bible Study* Galatians *and coauthor (with James Nyquist) of* Leading Bible Discussions: Revised Edition *(all from IVP).*